For my children, Josh, Zeb, and Heather, and
for my granddaughter, Alayna—with love.

C.D.B.

© 2001 Broadman & Holman Publishers
Nashville, Tennessee
All rights reserved.

Scripture taken from the HOLY BIBLE, NEW INTERNATIONAL READER'S VERSION™,
Copyright ©1995, 1996, 1998 by International Bible Society. Used by permission of
Zondervan Publishing House. All rights reserved.

Printed in U.S.A.
ISBN: 0-8054-2166-1

**Library of Congress Cataloging-in-Publication Data**

Better, Cathy Drinkwater.
  Excuse me! / poem by Cathy Drinkwater Better ; illustrated by Nancy Johnston.
    p. cm.
  Summary: Rhyming text explains the need for please and thank you and other examples
of good manners.
  ISBN 0-8054-2166-1 (hardcover)
  1. Etiquette for children and teenagers. [1. Etiquette. 2. Conduct of life.] I. Johnston,
Nancy, 1955- ill. II. Title.

BJ1857.C5 B399 2001
395.1'22--dc21

                                                                    99-055253

1 2 3 4 5  05 04 03 02 01

# Excuse Me!

Poem by
Cathy Drinkwater Better

Illustrated by
Nancy Johnston

BROADMAN & HOLMAN PUBLISHERS

What do you do
when you must say,

AAACHO

when a sneeze li

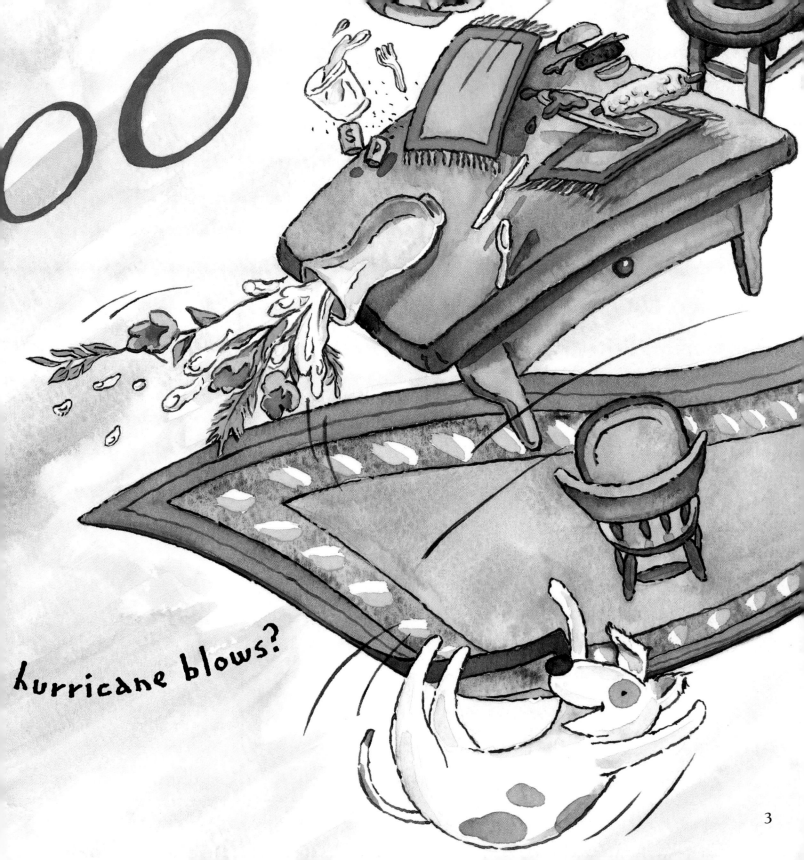

hurricane blows?

3

Don't stand on your head,
or go jump on the bed—
Say, "Excuse me"
(and cover your nose)!

*Train a child in the way he should go. When he is old,*
*he will not turn away from it. Proverbs 22:6*

RRRROAR

And what do you say
if someone's in your way?
Do you act like a lion
and roar?

Do you tickle
and lick them,
or take glue
and stick them?
Try, "Pardon me"—
that's what
manners are for!

*Be kind and tender to one another. Forgive each other, just as God forgave you because of what Christ has done. Ephesians 4:32*

9

If you have
a wrapper
from a Chocolate
Chip Zapper,
do you drop it
as you walk down
the street?

Just scrunch it up tight
and with all of your might,
sink a "trashball" from
seventeen feet!

*You made human beings the rulers over all that your hands have created. You put everything under their control. Psalm 8:6*

If you can't get your way
when you go out to play,
do you cry,
do you whine,
do you pout?

Do you take
your ball home
and just sit
all alone?
Go on and play—
that's what
teamwork's about!

And if Mom's
on the phone,
do you whimper
and moan?

Do you jump in her face
and make noise?

19

Do you suck on your toes
and put spoons
on your nose—
or wait patiently and
play with your toys?

*Children, obey your parents in everything.*
*That pleases the Lord.* Colossians 3:20

Good manners are easy!
You know, life can be breezy
if we make them a habit we share.

our good manners that prove that we care!

*Here is the command God has given us. Anyone who loves God must also love his brothers and sisters. 1 John 4:21*

25